Mrs White Had A Fright

And Other Songs And Chants

D0494625

Acknowledgements

Every effort has been made to obtain permission to reproduce copyright material but there may be cases where we have been unable to trace a copyright holder. The publisher apologizes for any such error and will be happy to correct any omission in future printings.

"This Is the Key" from OXFORD BOOK OF POETRY FOR CHILDREN. Reprinted by permission of Oxford University Press

"Piggy on the Railway" and "Moses" from I SAW ESAU edited by Iona and Peter Opie, illustrated by Maurice Sendak. Published 1992 by Walker Books Ltd, London

"Jelly on a Plate" and "Christopher Columbus" from HERE COMES MOTHER GOOSE edited by Iona Opie, illustrated by Rosemary Wells. Published 1999 by Walker Books Ltd, London

"Giant" from THE RED AND WHITE SPOTTED HANDKERCHIEF by Tony Mitton. © 2000 Tony Mitton

"Witch, Witch" by Rose Fyleman reprinted by permission of the Society of Authors as the Literary Representative of the Estate of Rose Fyleman

"Witch, Witch" from FIFTY-ONE NEW NURSERY RHYMES by Rose Fyleman. © 1931, 1932 Doubleday, a Division of Bantam Doubleday Dell Publishing Group Inc. Used by permission of Random House Children's Books, a Division of Random House, Inc.

"I Am Boj" © Adrian Mitchell. Available in BALLOON LAGOON AND THE MAGIC ISLANDS OF POETRY published by Orchard Books 1997. Reprinted by permission of PFD on behalf of Adrian Mitchell. Educational Health Warning! Adrian Mitchell asks that none of his poems are used in connection with any exams whatsoever.

"For Mary and her Kitten" and "The Tide in the River" © Eleanor Farjeon from SILVER SAND AND SNOW published by Michael Joseph. Reprinted by permission of David Higham Associates

"The Seagull's Song" from COWS MOO, CARS TOOT! by June Crebbin. © 1995 June Crebbin, published by Viking

"In the Barn" from THE ANIMAL WALL. © Gillian Clarke, published by Pont Books 1999

First published 2001 by Walker Books Ltd
87 Vauxhall Walk, London SE11 5HJ

This edition published 2007 for Index Books Ltd

4 6 8 10 9 7 5 3

This selection © 2001 CLPE/LB Southwark
Individual poems © as noted in acknowledgements
Illustrations © 2001 Judith Allibone

This book has been typeset in Adobe Caslon

Printed in China

All rights reserved

British Library Cataloguing in Publication Data:
a catalogue record for this book is
available from the British Library

ISBN 978-0-7445-6879-0

www.walkerbooks.co.uk

Mrs White Had A Fright
And Other Songs And Chants

Selected by Myra Barrs and Sue Ellis

Illustrated by Judith Allibone

WALKER BOOKS

AND SUBSIDIARIES

LONDON • BOSTON • SYDNEY • AUCKLAND

THIS IS THE KEY

This is the key of the kingdom:

In that kingdom there is a city.

In that city there is a town.

In that town there is a street.

In that street there is a lane.

In that lane there is a yard.

In that yard there is a house.

In that house there is a room.

In that room there is a bed.

On that bed there is a basket.

In that basket there are some flowers.

Flowers in a basket.

Basket on the bed.

Bed in the room.

Room in the house.

House in the yard.

Yard in the lane.

Lane in the street.

Street in the town.

Town in the city.

City in the kingdom.

Of the kingdom this is the key.

Traditional

LONDON BELLS

Oranges and lemons,

Say the bells of St Clement's.

Two sticks and an apple,

Say the bells at Whitechapel.

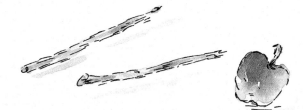

Kettles and pans,

Say the bells at St Anne's.

You owe me five farthings,

Say the bells of St Martin's.

When will you pay me?

Say the bells at Old Bailey.

When I grow rich,

Say the bells at Shoreditch.

Pray when will that be?

Say the bells at Stepney.

I'm sure I don't know,

Says the great bell at Bow.

Traditional

PIGGY ON THE RAILWAY

Piggy on the railway, picking up stones,

Up came an engine and broke Piggy's bones.

"Oh!" said Piggy, "that's not fair."

"Oh!" said the driver, "I don't care."

Traditional

JELLY ON A PLATE

Jelly on a plate,
Jelly on a plate,
Wibble, wobble, wibble, wobble,
Jelly on a plate.

Sausage in a pan,
Sausage in a pan,
Frizzle, frazzle, frizzle, frazzle,
Sausage in a pan.

Baby on the floor,
Baby on the floor,
Pick him up, pick him up,
Baby on the floor.

Traditional

GIANT

Great, big giant
like a great, fat lump.

Great, big boots
go thump, thump, thump.

Great, big bottom
as heavy as a hill.

Great, big belly
So difficult to fill.

Tiny, little brain
in a great, big head.

Great, big giant,
we wish you were dead!

Tony Mitton

WITCH, WITCH

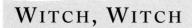

"Witch, witch, where do you fly?" ...
"Under the clouds and over the sky."

"Witch, witch, what do you eat?" ...
"Little black apples from Hurricane Street."

"Witch, witch, what do you drink?" ...
"Vinegar, blacking, and good red ink."

"Witch, witch, where do you sleep?" ...
"Up in the clouds where pillows are cheap."

Rose Fyleman

CHRISTOPHER COLUMBUS

Christopher Columbus
was a very great man,
He sailed to America
in an old tin can.
The can was greasy,
And it wasn't very easy,
And the waves grew higher,
and higher,
and higher.

Traditional

MOSES

Moses supposes his toeses are roses,

But Moses supposes erroneously.

For Moses he knowses his toeses aren't roses,

As Moses supposes his toeses to be.

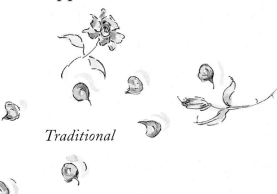

Traditional

ENDLESS CHANT

"Who put the overalls in Mrs Murphy's chowder?"

Nobody answered, so she said it all the louder:

"Who put the overalls in Mrs Murphy's chowder?"

Nobody answered, so she said it all the louder:

"Who put the overalls in Mrs Murphy's chowder?"

Nobody answered, so she said it all the louder:

"Who put the overalls in Mrs Murphy's chowder?"

Nobody answered, so she said it all the louder:

"Who put the overalls in Mrs Murphy's chowder?"

Nobody answered, so she said it all the louder:

"Who put the overalls in Mrs Murphy's chowder?"

Nobody answered, so she said it all the louder:

"Who put the overalls in Mrs Murphy's chowder?"

Nobody answered, so she said it all the louder...

Traditional

I Am Boj

(To be shouted, in the voice of a terrible giant,

at children who wake early)

I am Boj
I crackle like the Wig of a Judge

   I am Boj
My eyes boil over with Hodge-Podge

   I am Boj
Organized Sludge and a Thunder-Wedge

   I am Boj
I am a Tower of solid Grudge

   I am Boj
The molten Centre, the cutting Edge

   I am Boj
From blackest Dudgeon I swing my Bludgeon

   I am Boj

Adrian Mitchell

FOR MARY AND HER KITTEN

The Kitten's in the Dairy!

Where's our Mary?

She isn't in the Kitchen,

She isn't at her Stitching,

She isn't at the Weeding,

The Brewing, or the Kneading!

Mary's in the Garden, walking in a Dream,

Mary's got her Fancies, and the Kitten's got the Cream.

Eleanor Farjeon

MINNIE AND WINNIE

Minnie and Winnie
    Slept in a shell.
Sleep, little ladies!
    And they slept well.

Pink was the shell within,
    Silver without;
Sounds of the great sea
    Wandered about.

Sleep, little ladies!
    Wake not soon!
Echo on echo
    Dies to the moon...

Alfred Lord Tennyson

There's a brown girl in the ring,
Tra-la-la-la-la.
There's a brown girl in the ring,
Tra-la-la-la-la.
A brown girl in the ring,
Tra-la-la-la-la,
For she's sweet like a sugar
And a plum, plum, plum.

Now show me your motion,
Tra-la-la-la-la,
Now show me your motion,
Tra-la-la-la-la,
Now show me your motion,
Tra-la-la-la-la.
For she's sweet like a sugar
And a plum, plum, plum.

Now hug and kiss your partner,
Tra-la-la-la-la,
Now hug and kiss your partner,
Tra-la-la-la-la.
Now hug and kiss your partner,
Tra-la-la-la-la.
For she's sweet like a sugar
And a plum, plum, plum.

Traditional

Mrs White Had a Fright

Mrs White had a fright,
in the middle of the night.
Saw a ghost, eating toast,
half-way up a lamp-post.

Mrs Black got the sack,
said she wasn't coming back.

Mrs Green saw the Queen,
on the television screen.

Mrs Brown went to town,
with her knickers hanging down.

Mrs Red went to bed,
and in the morning she was dead.

Traditional

FLOP, CLONK, BUMP, ZOOM

Floppily, floppier, floppity, flop, flop.
Flippily, flippier, flippity, flip, flip.

Clonkily, clonkier, clonkity, clonk, clonk.
Clinkily, clinkier, clinkity, clink, clink.

Sloshily, sloshier, sloshity, slosh, slosh.
Splashily, splashier, splashity, splash, splash.

Bumpily, bumpier, bumpity, bump, bump.
Boomily, boomier, boomity, boom, boom.
Zoomily, zoomier, zoomity, zoom, zoom.

James Berry

WHERE DO YOU SLEEP?

The green worm sleeps in silk,

The turtle sleeps in sand,

And the bluebird sleeps in a feather bed,

The yak prefers to stand.

The white lamb sleeps in wool,

The ermine sleeps in fur,

But the monkey sleeps in his mommy's arms,

All warm and close to her.

William Engvick

THE ANSWERS

"When did the world begin and how?"

I asked a lamb, a goat, a cow.

"What's it all about and why?"

I asked a hog as he passed by.

"How will the whole thing end, and when?"

I asked a duck, a goose, a hen,

And I copied all the answers too:

A quack, a honk, an oink, a moo!

Robert Clairmont

THE SEAGULL'S SONG

Oh, I do like to be beside the seaside,

I do like to be beside the sea,

I do like to soar above a seaside town,

See the boats in the harbour bobbing up and down.

Oh, I do like to be beside the seaside,

There is nowhere that I would rather be,

I can perch on sailing-ships,

Grab a meal of fish and chips,

Beside the seaside, beside the sea.

June Crebbin

THE TIDE IN THE RIVER

The tide in the river,
> The tide in the river,
The tide in the river runs deep.
> I saw a shiver
> Pass over the river
As the tide turned in its sleep.

Eleanor Farjeon

IN THE BARN

In the old oak beam
is the rustling forest

In the fork of the roof
is the pigeon's nest

In the mound of hay
is the summer meadow

In the web-winged bat
is the flittering shadow

In the fox and the owl
are the night-bringers

In the gaps between stones
are the wind's fingers

In the glittering frost
are the cold stars

In the cracks in the roof
are silver bars

In the puddle on the floor
is the moon's face

In the thawing stream
is spring's voice

In the creak of the door
is the swallow's cry

In the hole in the shutter
is the sun's eye

Gillian Clarke

OTHER READ ME BOOKS

Read Me Beginners are simple rhymes and
stories ideal for children learning to read.

Read Me Story Plays are dramatized versions of favourite
stories, written for four or more voices to share.